AF427564

SHADOW CONFESSIONS

RAW VERSION

SHELL SHERWOOD

poetry and reflections

ISBN: 979-8-9955021-0-4

Cover photo by Rachel Hilton

sherwoodforestpress.com

For those who have navigated the turbulent currents of
darkness and light.

Acknowledgements

There are several people in my life without whom this book would never have come to be.

To my warriors (Jackson, Gus, Patrick, and Carmella), who inspire me to stay resilient and whimsical every day.

To my Moms Who Write tribe (Allie, Amber, Allison, Sarah, Emily, Jill, and Brigid), who have supported my dreams in every phase of life. A special thanks to Abby for helping me edit and design.

To my sister Rachel, for editing, contributing, and being my art soulmate.

To my love, William, who sees me for who I am and encourages and champions every crazy idea I dare to dream.

From the bottom of my heart, thank you.

I always thought
the sporadic verses in my mind
the ones
that transform my thoughts
into spurs
were just remnants of memories
floating carelessly
violently maturing into electric dust
settling in cavities
while I licked the wounds they left.

I never thought
to put these verses to paper
to breathe life
into the shadows I recoiled from
grant mercy
upon the words that internally lashed
a second chance
for redemption and apologies
to shine
perhaps enough to dull their blades.

Phase 1:
Descend

unconscious vice

I used to be a fearless girl, until my blood began to run
welcoming darkness like a smothering clock
a ticking time bomb clamping on a schedule
around my mind, radiating through my body
crossing wires in sacred fields

it starts with a prick—a twinge of uncomfortable air
creeping to a roll before engulfing every image
that graces my sight, all that I've ever known
anything my trembling fingers can grasp
a piercing twinkle between tears
a heaviness greater than I'm ever prepared for

this force is not an ally
not quite an enemy, in respect
rather a reflection of every dark intention
terrifying, with the gift of predictability

my heart begs for mercy
my soul cries for release
I have so much to do
  I was so close to finishing
    I need more time
      just one more day
        one more day, please
          please...

by the time I feel its presence, my mind
has already been ensnared
compressed among mechanical inclinations
of malice
to a degree I will never comprehend
or deserve

on exit, it leaves a stain of fear
festering thoughts of what life would be like
if this reality was infinite
if the vice clamped and ceased to recoil
nothing left but darkness
views of hazy greys over rainbow treasures
muffled sounds replacing music and laughter

but more surprisingly
fear of its absence

for what if the vice vanishes, indefinitely
leaving light and crystal visions
lullabies sweetening my ears
sunny days among dreary skies

where will my creations come from then?
can I truly be myself without them?
maybe I've never really met myself
without them.

blind woman

there's a woman I am scared of
pulsing fear through every cortex
pulling clouds to smear my mind
flashing lights behind my eyes

in a rage, I see her looming there
with swelling smoke and fire breath
compassion left to roam astray
callous against frayed loyalty

she spits her words so fiercely
with scant filters to protect
yet ever so quickly warps again
into hands I crave to hold.

the wall

I know you hated the words on the wall
you said I was a 'crazy person'
cooped up in a room, scripting nonsense on paint
and maybe you were right

but those words were anchors
among the chaos of deep shadows
in the heart of a girl
too fragile to make sense of them

the words never left
never grew, never changed
I controlled every letter
the tone of each smoldering line
handpicked, scrolled with purpose
striking chords on solemn times
they failed to vanish on abandoned nights
or tip their nose to curiosity
or shame with silence for naive mistakes
of those I'm sure there were many
they survived despite their photo neighbors
ripping and fraying around them
warping from one face to another
to none
no faces left to frame the words
of a 'crazy person'

the words were a respite
from the mayhem in my mind
smudged along swerving lines
stained with tears of moscato rage
perhaps appreciated most
by the poetic greats and creative muses
a bit of genius mixed with madness
laced with courage mimicking mania

I finished the wall shortly before I left
an escape to the ocean
where these loyal words could never follow
cinched by coffee carpet threads
with a final free-written verse
a rotten cherry topping to a chapter
I hoped never to repeat

I can't remember any of the words now
you painted over them as soon as I left

thank you.

tainted romantic

some of our inner critics
are worse than others—
      tumultuous, smothering
      like crushing flower stems
      before they ever had a chance
      to meet the sun...

some of our inner critics
are worse than others—
      tumultuous, smothering
      like negating your heart
      before it ever had a chance
      to embrace true love.

your name recoils my insides
sludge in the pit of a barrel

accompanying a strange shoulder
of temporary warmth

sometimes bare
rarely given a thought

for the syllables of the sludge will mold
too frequently to treasure

the colors of your eyes warp
with ever-changing scents of skin

around a collective stable aura
of bleeding black

protective against my worst demons
dismissive of my strengths

attempts at securing
star-crossed fantasies

I think I'll go to Boston

what am I even doing here?
this is not what I signed up for

blushed and cat-eyed, dolled up in a suit of tweed
my naive, size one figure gleaming
picking at the fresh cubicle pencils
flitting with the edges of a manual
waiting for my files, waiting to do good
watching as the office never stopped
       workers rushing, typing, scripting, shifting
       in and out of doors, in and out of crisis
I couldn't wait, couldn't wait to spark change...

not this

I had dreamed of moving to the city
singing Augustana, with my cat's
blaring meows echoing against the rattles
of boxes bursting with momentos
sixteen hours of pure anticipation
a cobblestone jungle awaiting my heels
the ocean breeze pining for this landlocked soul
icing my blood with just one dip
I was home (finally) a place to start anew
to have a real purpose, perhaps find love...

what love is this?
this was not part of the plan

I had left my town, to run away in a sense
though few will I admit that to
from the pain of failing friendships
from the shame of all the mistakes I made
midnight love that never stuck
liquid courage staining my tongue
barbed remarks I couldn't retract
heart sung games through lawless eyes
the darkness telling me to quit
  while you're ahead
  while you're alone
it whispered
of broken hearts and hope
I ran from all of that to this...

not to this
not toward the black mirror I had been dreading
this
this place...

there's never any sleep here
there's never any sleep
my eyes have sunk into my head
popping out on springs
only when mandates refused to cease
chasing people through the streets
        through the veins of nightmares
            in this city of my dreams

the phone never stops
the phone is alive
hitting the pillow to dart back up
I never even change my clothes
my foulness slinks out painted doors
        to save a life before the dawn
        to talk her out of final decisions
        to monitor self-mutilation by phone
            down twisted alleys and shady streets

her hidden needles in my seat
his buried loathing of his soul
her bloody lip stained porcelain cheeks
and when caffeine was not enough
(it had to be enough, it must)
I'd drown in all their unsolved pain
        if I could manage to wake myself
            enough to recall it...

what am I even doing here?
this is not what I signed up for
how am I supposed to save them

when their shadows
are eating mine alive?

rooted

there's a tree in the woods
that never greens
it adorns a hue of burnt orange
blending only once a year
before escaping to the forest floor

I feel for this sapling
dormant in disguise
constantly pretending, yearning
for just a vein of green to fit
one speck of traditional color

not this year, my friend
stained again with nothing but a reminder
of the darker days to come
warm and yet an eyesore
for sweethearts of summer bliss

she's too rooted
too embedded in her soil
to seek souls who can value
the burden and beauty
of everlasting dying leaves.

cold noodles

my stomach felt as if it could wretch
despite any substance I slid inside
and yet I chose—
       among all other comfort foods
       that could have padded the belly
       warmed my nerves
something as harsh as
cold day-old noodles

anticipating your response to the life I discovered
unemployed, immature, unaware
I choked on my next move—
       how to parent
       how to guide
       a fragile being
I couldn't even bring myself to heat up these
cold day-old noodles

I rehearsed my discovery in the purple shower steam
catching every word to morph into a bubble of hope
to present memorably—
       a surprise cake
       a hidden stick
       a bump drawn in the sand
unable to predict your demeanor, my legs wobbled like
cold day-old noodles

I confessed—

> without a show
> without a prop
> without a second

to even breathe

draped in a musty towel
my hair dripping on matted carpet
where the stink bugs marched in haunting lines
to swarm behind a vintage chair
torn from the beatup car you cherished
more than my announcement

I pretended to mirror your instant
disappointment
despite the taunting lack of shame
I left you there in shock and despair
and every emotion that wafted between

I snuck into a robe and down the stairs
1am starvation calling
to savor what was left of my joy
in peace
and fill my growing belly with
cold day-old…two-day-old…noodles.

red flag evermore

it's a strange relationship
professional only and yet
I know her every desire

her stagnant truths and florid lies
the ugliest secrets of her past
the terrors that keep her up at night
wandering the streets in search of love
belonging
or simply a night of warmth without having to charge

it's impossible to spend so much time with someone
and not think of them from time to time
or recall their worst nightmares
sworn to secrecy
locked in your brain along with your own
a pact she never knew she made

I think of her
when I pass the house with peeling cedar shakers
and drooping gutters bearing witness
to the virtue he stole from her
never to be restored, not that he'd try

sometimes I wake in the dead of the night
to phantom calls that sound alarms
to rescue her from the mistakes she made

to rescue her from her own dark thoughts
to be the soothing memory in her mind
swimming among a sea of filth

a swelling dump
layered by the wrath of others
of family members, doctors, providers, friends
blurred by pills and needles and lies
leaving only the shame to warm

she didn't even own a bag
the ones she had, she gave away
to someone else she tried to buy
she always had to buy her love
despite the confidence in her jaded step
and the innocent path her tears would fall
in congested, lonely hospital hallways
when the beds were scarce and she no stranger

the day I left, she stared through me
with predictable wells in her eyes
as I was one of the *good ones gone*
relief struck cold in the pit of my stomach
hardened with guilt for feeling this way
I really was just another number
in a line of people
she was trying to buy love from—

I embraced her grease-filled hair
as she was called away
the barricade closed behind her
and she was physically gone
mentally cemented.

three plus hours too late

demanding cells to move my legs
to rid them of pesky pins and needles
replaying priceless events that unfolded
behind a superficial curtain
routine procedure, perfect birth
perfect weight, perfect cry
perfect, perfect, perfect, so they said
so—where is he?

still parked in a recovery room, frozen
with a rackety anquished woman, weeping
after taking a fall from a curb or a step
surrounded by loved ones with genuine worry
consoling her body and soul, sincerely
like soothing a terrified infant after birth
from the cold, unnaturally sterile air
like mine was, so—where is he?

I still lie alone, in spite of myself
a fresh, hellish slice I have yet to feel
a body pulled through stubborn skin
with no romantic notion, as promised
a little stuck, he sung behind masks
shuffling vital organs in pans
caving my world in to free a head grown
into my rib cage, just so—where is he?

his father flees from floor to floor
a war with an unknown technical beast
screens flashing fury with every scan
not a patient, no match, not a patient
three plus hours of restless assessments
unsuccessful wiggles and empty questions
who is this? this lady! she had a baby? where's the baby?!
the golden question of the day is: where is he?

a swollen nurse rushes in with a bundle
a baby boy swaddled to near suffocation
tomato-cheeked wails invite many strange eyes
to narrow directly at my vacant chest
frigid hands rip open my gown
to shoot out an insult and slap on a shield
shoving his screeching face violently in

there he is, he's here—three plus hours too late

three plus hours of isolation was long enough
to cause confusion in my mind
the kind that makes a mother question
everything
in the most dangerous of ways
not forever, at least
in this instance
just three plus months.

postpartum

like stones on a sunrise
I fall heavy on your eyes
burning the memories
that infamously haunt
your dreams.

crackers & milk

electric shocks
shoot fiercely through my breasts
I'd massage them
but my hands are caked in peanut butter
and cracker salt

a late-night habit formed
out of fear
of smothering my child beneath my weight
at the only time I find joy in nurturing
from my own body

an experience I yearned for
dreamed of
labeled a nuisance by jealous voices
whose opinions
are never silent

rushers, of a sacred process
pure intimacy
a moment for just two souls
blood running deep
in separate streams

every time I think I'm close
to mending gaping wounds
broken from circumstances
out of my control
they're severed from impatience

selfish desires
grabby hands
snatching before the last drop settles
gulping cheeks barely deflated
my heart hollows with every steal

so I savor
these witching hour moments
as the electric shocks subside
I sleeve the peanut smears from my face
lick the salt from my fingertips

before setting
to burp this gentle creature
now covered in debris
debating in darkness
if the bits I swiped away were

soggy crackers or tears.

midnight stranger

there's a demon in our bed
my love, you're lost again in dreams
hidden behind wandering eyes
puzzled looks, muttered commands

I rescued you
one summer night
when steps of wonder possessed your toes
those clouded eyes saw nothing more
than a monster looking to feast

come back to me, my love
come back
return to the soul you left on these sheets
I know my face may not be grace
but nothing is as terrifying
as the night devil behind your eyes.

blood count

a drip
unexpected, down your nose
over your plump lips
smearing your smile
quickly trailing down your chin
a micro puddle
at your feet
I can't remember cleaning it, though
I doubt it was the first to grace this sterile floor

it's too white

your eyes
iced over in confusion from our worry
I stand frozen to the hospital floor
did I step in the puddle?
did I smear it out the door?
down the hall to the room
where metal cages pose as beds

I know I grabbed you thoughtlessly
without a tissue in my hand
next to the boy with a rolling cart
a shiny head beneath a wrap
and a bandaged hand to grip a pole
dispensing life after dripping poison

I want so badly to take you home
but we don't know why

      your body's failing
      your pallete's bruised
      your stomach's revolting
      your nose is flowing

your life source
pours too freely, love
refusing to cake and clot
the people here are angels
but this is no club I wish to join

and yet
the least I could have done
was left it as sterile and white

as I found it.

late April

I've never felt more blinded
than the day she rang my phone
back to back
a loved one's cry for

       emergency

       urgency

       disaster

I suppose it was rather fitting

I let her pass her message
I'm sure you already know now…
a confession from a stranger
introduced amid

       hatred

       betrayal

       confusion

she claimed to know you—*know you*

your attempted foul play lies
pierced my heart straight through
you warned me to expect her voice
but omitted

       the context

       the story

       the truth

uncovering a buried pattern

I never knew you were a *bad* liar

I never knew you *were* a liar.

seen not heard

tucked behind paper doors
condescending eyes darting over warm plates
slinking around the hearts at your table
for failing silent expectations

unwanted noise
ignites true character
I've found

my respect for you
fizzled when the curtains fell
when your soundproof lies
attempted to hush away love

love you invited to this home.

ancestorial insomnia

I always wonder if she felt like this
    did she pace the halls as I do
    in worn disheveled carpet patterns
    bubbled popcorn kernels
    the same threads
    I used to lay my face upon
    amid lonely childhood dramas
    picking absentmindedly
    at their plumpness

    did she cry as she roamed
    regretting chosen words
    a temper that never ceased
    did it overwhelm her
    in the kitchen by the stove
    against the dusty food-trapped crack
    I can never seem to clean

I find myself frozen here
fixated on every lost morsel
caked and crumbling amid the gap
my mistakes
all piled up and compacted together
until a greasy residue spills
forcing them forward to the tile
where they can no longer be ignored

I wipe feverishly at the stains
scraping, scratching, lifting what I can
before my children can snatch the crumbs
of poisonous insults
disguised as love
sugared in denial
to be reserved and rebranded
as care—leftovers

but her stove was always so clean
streak-free
the glossy plastic rarely dulled
I never recall a stain or mark out of place
and boy, did I look

where did she hide her crumbs?
did she have them?

I always was the untidy one.

morning survivor

the morning was born pure
silent snow dusting my nose
melting on swollen cheeks
the forest
not yet bustling
with squirrels and chipmunks
woodpeckers and finches
still in slumber
despite the ascending sun
striking fiery chords
straight through their hearts
pumping divine blood
to detonate the dawn

they were simply still
at peace

not a sound to be heard
nor vibration to tremble
just the struggle
of my own breath
pining for warmth
grateful
that my midnight torment
failed to disturb them.

wishes for angel babies

I never met anyone who wished
for angel babies
save for her

the one with endless ringlets
a sideways contagious smile
who conceived through force and malice
no safe home
she prayed for blood and the pinch
of life to cease
run between her legs
so she wouldn't have to make
the choice
she knew would take a piece of her
forever
2am she called me weeping
of hell and murderous tendencies
I cooed her back to sleep
or so she pretended
like a blind night dove

as if I had the right to speak
as if I knew what I should say
barely legal
barely functioning
arriving with empty hands

no
no one
not the lucky ones like us
wish for angel babies
but you did

at least once
out loud.

splatters of shame

misplaced outrage surging
as my body barreled down to the basement
the hammering of my heart
allowing my chest to succumb
my shoulders taut with disappointment

I grasped your arm
so soft, so disobedient
folded your plump body into my own
the weight you bore was too heavy to chance
my stubbornness, too great to challenge

I stamped each stair
with a force meant to split the wood
beneath my bare feet
the stickiness of pandemic summer heat
soaking through my calluses

I ignored your cry of defiance
lasting briefly amid my childish fit
as if the world was over in my mind
for reasons I can't remember
of little importance in the grand scheme

I heard your brother's piercing screams
from the kitchen, over toys
or crayons or food or anything
it never took much for a scream in this house
at least back in those times

I tried to dull the noise with my stomps
and the blaring hum of the dehumidifier
suppressing my unconscious warning signs
don't. slow down. stop.
I persisted—I slipped

I couldn't ignore your cry this time
the blood was loud enough
on the step
on the wall
on my hands
I wished it had been mine

every so often I catch myself staring
at the scar on your bottom lip
a strike of white that shines when you smile
your twinkling eyes melting surrounding hearts
while I bury myself in the shame of its origin
the bloody staircase.

speck

I saw a speck of dirt, you shrugged
the dirt became a film of dust
I tried to feather off the top
but something tacky, oddly rough
had tethered to the pesky bit
I begged you to be rid of it
you turned your shoulder cold away
you couldn't see the speck that lay

the dust began to melt to muck
beneath the wrath of August sun
beating harshly on window sills
scarred by talons, a dripping pun
it smeared along the cream-brushed walls
who claimed they were pristine at all?
now marked with unappealing stains
carved red with unfamiliar names

I bit my fist and called to you
to rectify this daunting scene
replace a molding, scathe the wall
craft an illusion it was clean
the cost of such was far too high
at least amid your fragile eyes
and so I watched the ooze drip more
till acid craters filled the floor

arriving with October's breeze
a warped and twisted crystal mess
I tried to kick and scrape it clear
with every tool that I possessed
cemented to the ground it stayed
still taunting me without parlay
my vacant hand outstretched to you
where only silent whispers blew

desperation dissolved my will
I picked each cross-grained jagged piece
while lifting flesh, lost nails and hope
still trembling on my hands and knees
devouring every cracking edge
but I too numb to feel a shred
I severed it to its last breath
were you around, or had you left?

a final prick disarms the beast
my pulsing nailbeds, bloodied black
start wading through the piles of waste
expecting triumph, stepping back
but though the speck could not be traced
crimson smudges remained in place
so deeply seared inside this home
it haunts me when the red bricks moan

my body fell, mere stagnant weight
drawn pasty white and frail at best
lie pounded down and drained complete
sinking matter forsook to rest
yet–

        presently you come equipped
        with gleaming tools upon your hip
        to mend the mess that I have made
        to mend the mess that I...wait—

I thought you couldn't see the speck?
you couldn't even see the speck
or did you see it after all
yielding, enough to see me fall?

descent initiated

a chronic pinch of dread
a nagging ache that grinds my brain
I visit it often
about once a month
but this time, it's not going away

I wake in it
feel my body melting into worry
before the sun can kiss my face
my heart tender from a loss
I have yet to discover

baby smiles warming my chest
are all that can resurrect me
until the turn of their cheek
whips icy air
cutting through my heart
like a million shards

I don't want to go to sleep
  I'm afraid of wasting time
I don't want to sleep too long
  I'm afraid of wasting time
I don't want the shadows to come
  I'm afraid they'll take my time

this hole I'm sinking into
is sucking my life reserves
from the stash I dig in
when all feels hopeless
the one I save for those I love
replacing it with dense remorse
of decisions made by chance and luck

ten years of guilt
pining for different waves
knowing I'd still sail them by choice
if given the chance to turn back time

maybe I could drop
a message in a bottle
to warn my future self
to overfill my bucket
before I begin.

home

there's no place like home
until it's not that

> once impenetrable walls
> turned to parchment
> slashed by frigid shoulders
> charred in defensive spats
> disintegrating
> with every projectile tear
> allowed to waste away
> in silent contempt
> jagged trails of pulpy paste
> smeared across loathing tiles

there's no place like home
until it's not that, anymore.

anxiety on ice

I pace the shadows you left
    that trickle down my spine
        icy crystals popping
            never sleeping
                never resting
                    a crack of fear
                        of impending doom

                        of life still here
                  to lock it away
              deep in my chest
            savoring the proof
        enough to return
      beneath my covers
until–

I can't shake it
    and so I creep
    in unison with darkness
    tiptoeing worn paths
    to breathe it in
a calming warmth

the crystals burst open
again
or
Good Morning.

reminisce

I knew you once
at the tip of darkened skies
where ideas flow lavishly
unapologetically

we embraced
like long-lost hearts often do
for moments, minutes at most
before you slunk away once more
to wherever it is you hide
when my mind needs strength
the most

the business of life begins once more

I'm left a breathless fool
an imposter
of the words I siphon my life from.

they're here

when nothing soothes anxious ties
the hollow clouds roaming my heart
can feel them lurk
waiting to feed
on any light that streams astray
on any hope that flees the night
they overtake each thought of wonder
'til the sunrise is too dense to penetrate
the darkness in my mind

that's when I know they're here

the shadows

consistent dawning
of my reality
or perhaps
an unveiling of the matrix

I've created.

Phase 2:
Abyss

rage stage #1: pressure

at the base of my neck
I sense it when it's near
my words flow freely when it arrives
but the desolation it carries can be
unbearable

people fail to fake sincerity
I bury pitiful cries for help

it feels as if a dagger has been
stolen from its sheath
a throbbing vacancy in my temple
begging to be filled
calmed by the chill of steel

if I only knew where to find the blade
to make this all go away

I've tried a few that didn't fit.

patchwork creature

ink splots blur a rounded head
the curve of a spine
the curl of a tail
under two hidden feet
but no face to gaze
yet I see it stare

it shimmers in the shadows
or perhaps it's sewn right in
disappearing when the glow
of the candle strikes the room
retracting from innocence
its disappearance
draws concern

I hold the candle onward
long enough to confirm defeat
not forever, just for now
in all honesty, its presence
while unsettling
fills my loneliness.

strings

my nails
could never grow long enough
to scathe the layer in my mind
that whispers putrid thoughts
telling me I'm worthless
singing my loved ones are better off
without my hand to hold
to hurt
inception dawning long ago
I never saw the strings till now
my days could be
as bright and lovely
without these fretful threads
but the narrative
traveling down these lines
swells and seeps
to veil any good

nevertheless
I tend to them with care.

madness theatre

spectators love to whisper

on my stage

maybe they're right

perhaps I *am* truly mad

that would explain my desire

for an encore.

that poor old soul
she lost her mind
it once was there—there!
on lyrical display
but left some time
nearing final breaths
when cheers erupted
and bodies rose
she smiled with recollection
of the words and songs
she sang with perfection
with faceless characters
sadly
the black curtain descended
engulfed her in madness
of the worst affair
like a twister in a storm
till all that was left
were anecdotes
lines in books
and stars on the horizon

peppermint soap

on a winter's night
my body deflects the warmth

I scald my skin
in hopes to reach my bones
the steam billowing around me
my blazing hide sizzling
droplets clinging to veiny walls
a rainforest aura
scaling slate grey paint

my eyes are as hazy
as the clouded mirrors
I fiercely swipe
to clear a portal
a road of remembrance
a glimpse of what it was
that ever warmed me
to begin with

but the mist
though thick and suffocating
does not speak
does not hold space
does not envelop me
in comforting false belief
not like the shadows

the shadows may be chilling
but at least they speak to me.

rage stage #2: infestation

at the summit of my heart
searing the perimeter
before striking like an arrow
to the tip of the shoulder
knifing downward to hit each curve
crawling up again
to weave its thorns
into every nerve beneath my skin
wreaking havoc in my veiny neck
while skillfully scaling through my ribs
to pry my chest wide open

exposing my flesh to the chill of the air

it's rarely simple enough
to sever the bond clean
to hold my hand steady enough
for this burn is ingrained in me
even when dormant
I sense its breath

if I cut away its entirety
I'm afraid of which parts
of my soul may break
consequently
and so I carve around the grain until
the numbness starts to spread.

haunting desires

I used to have this recurring dream
of desiring to be covered in blood
I won't pretend it wasn't morbid
but it's so

from head to toe, like Carrie, but content
maybe from an act of love or courage
overcoming something spectacular
unworldly
the edges of the scenes are blurry at best

when I close my eyes on shadowy days
I can still feel the thickness in my hair
slowly streaming down my cheeks
blanketing my arms in sheets
encompassing everything
as I turn my forearms to distribute
not to be greedy, but equal

I've never known if it was mine
or someone else's
an enemy, a lover, a demon, a friend
I've had this dream since childhood
and at one point, I believed it to be heroic
a premonition

as the years have passed
the inkling in the vision hasn't ceased
but I have to wonder
if this terror in my brain is really
as celebratory as I've yearned it to be

a scene in a book I have yet to write
an ungodly future
a gallant rescue
past life memories
or perhaps more likely
most concerning
desire

desire to feel
comforted
validated

warm
I can never get warm
here.

parasite

you infect in the shadows
crawl, feast on blooded tissue
beneath the skin you rot away
claiming space that doesn't belong

to you

with every nibble you sink the ship
sailing towards the future
of these courageous boys
whose love extends further
than the deepest crevices of life
where only stardust and magic reside
I'd sleep if it was not for the likes

of you

a purposeless existence
I could quite possibly feel again
if you were to shrivel up to ash
layers of fine particles
drifting up through my pores
cast into the wind
never to lay eyes on again

a delight.

don't blink

sleepless nights
spark life among the shadows
I see them everywhere

slinking, creeping
slithering in corners
huddled over door frames
whipping, spinning like spiders
but bulky, menacing
they sense when I'm near
and I them
but never quite in unison
they creep into my vision
premeditated
without opportune time to escape
while I catch them off guard
witnessing their wallowing
in my bed with the covers strewn over my eyes
through the woods during 3 am cracker binges
in the alleyways of closing city streets
on highways darkened by towering pines
lit only by passing hazy orange lamps

I feel them first
before their crippled bodies
trudge down the parkway
venturing somewhere close to home
they jump without sympathy
sparking tightness in my ribs
my mind's a wreck
forever deciphering reality from the darkness
juggling the tricks of tired nights
where shadows flutter my lashes
whispering corrosive wishes
begging me to let them win

the rested like to gawk and turn away from such claims and yet I
ask what your reaction would be if the shadows graced your
door? suffice to say, they probably already have—

perhaps you blinked.

vultures

the turkey vultures circle in unison
as I lay motionless in the grass
high above the silver treetops
black omens defying blue skies

three, circling
swooping, swirling
skimming crispy leaves
to make their presence known
investigating movement below
certifying the death of intended prey

I lie and listen to distant giggles
of my three resilient warriors
exploring the surrounding woods
their shrieks do not frighten the birds of prey
that eye me from the sky above

I wonder how long I should keep this up
I wonder how long I *can* keep this up
holding air, too scared to breathe
not because of these circling birds

on days like this
with only a few moments of reflection
my body is too overwhelmed to move
too shocked with peace
to know what to do with it
time that is growing shorter with every second

they consciously flee, disappointed
they must have heard the cranking wheels
the turmoil inside this crowded head
signals of life still present

or were my thoughts
just too toxic for their taste?

picky birds.

love limits

unconditional love
takes a toll that no one speaks of
like a boulder placed shrewdly
upon my heart

mountains blocking foreign energy
from invasion
a fortress to protect
divert
regardless of the good intention
a mass
sometimes more than I can bear

there is no unlimited supply
of unconditional love
not for people
like me.

rage stage #3: collapse

upon my collarbone
heavy enough to puncture
when I weep
bowing under vibrations
rising up from panicked lungs
never warping despite the abundant tears
filling valleys beneath its roots
too profound to shudder

compacted hysteria bedding down

the efforts forth to catch a breath
fall short with bladed tongues
ricocheting down my throat
stirring among the acid

like wood, it splinters
shredding tissue as it sways
like metal, it leaches
metallic liquid stains my tongue.

cloud pillow nightmares

sheets threaded so delicately soft
should never be wasted in the hands
of a soul this wretched

his porcelain cheek should be stroked
each touch a kiss upon his skin
whispering familiar melodies
that whisks his mind to sleep
on the golden waves, she wove for him
that dance upon spring winds
delivering the last of crystal flakes
to the tip of his rounded nose
like a marble made to be stolen
pocketed away by those he loves
making his slim white teeth reveal a laugh
that echoes through your heart

but—

there can't be an echo
when the teeth are bared
in a piercing screech
and the nose is hidden frightfully
beneath the cotton cloud
where dreams are supposed to live
yet only terrorizing nightmares reign
and the melodies sound muffled
butted up against his cheek
of porcelain perfection.

faultline

I'm sorry for the tear-soaked pillow beside you. I was reminiscing of the younger years when it hit me they were gone. when it hit me that the mistakes I made are cemented in the past. the damages irreversible at best and only sheer, ornamental bandages can be placed. that you will never forget the hate I spewed and hurtful words I crafted. the raging monster storming towards you. the one I've since defeated (or tried). there will never be a time when you look at me and cease to recall the hideous form I took. when I thought control was love and obedience was respect and the words of the innocent held little value compared to the guides who use them as weapons. you will always see the monster. I have become your first shadow and it haunts me within my own. and so my tears will continue to flow among the fleece as I curve the salty streams to avoid disturbing the peace you experience away from me.

it's not your fault.

racing fatigue
a tired
so burdensome
you can see it in the air
it waves indifferently
across aluminum blinds
and ripples in screens
blips of light and pulsing streams
beating steadily down
on the dented hood
of the van I escape to
when the air solidifies on my skin
quickly thickening into tar
tingling the bones under my cheek
and I need to speed it up
before it cures me to this seat
and so I drive.

lies in the sand

it's come to my attention that the poet in me
may only show her face out of desperation
afraid of eviction from the timeless wrath
my mind holds so tightly around her throat

in moments of bliss
she is released and unattended to
forgotten
pushed to the bottom of the pit
just a grain of sand drowning
in a sandy abyss
of bland, unrecognizable attributes
no verses to dance on
cursing my happiness

when chaos and darkness dawn
she rises
spewing from isolation
to rule the mind she once held in vain
weaving her magical words
among the entanglements of sorrow
pain and loss and numbness
feeding off the torment
of this shadowy attention
revengeful verses birthed from solitude

if she would only listen
I'd tell her she was free
a grain unconstrained
along the shoreline of my emotions
possessing the will to speak
whenever she pleases

we both know that's not true.

rainbow bubble nightmare

the silent echo of my heartbeat
is deafening
transforming into a jackhammer
that lives near my skull
chiseling without interruption
the faintest of sounds
reverberating each nerve
shredding them away
piece by piece

I try to fill the space with noise
but the words only drown
without context
I press my crooked spine
against frigid bamboo boards
and stare at soot-filled ceilings
taking in a loneliness
so intense
my breath takes the form
of rainbow bubbles

I mold them into transparent creatures
like when I was young
iridescent delights, dancing
in the absence of human words
so distracted—

replicating with ease
until my perception is nothing
but soapy swirls
that divert from the ache
of a jackhammer silence

you arrive again
armed with more muted weapons
blatant, callous movements
through a *home*
as if I don't exist

you stare at my floating words
among a sea of silent bubbles
bouncing askew
never reaching your ears
instead of marveling at their complexity
or ignoring their existence

you pop them

igniting a glittery mist
that stuffs my nose
invades my lashes
pummels my irises

still—

I'd close my eyes
to protect myself
I would

but I'm petrified
of silence
paired with darkness.

rage stage #4: acceptance

I'm no foreigner
to this monster
decomposing my body
one fit at a time
a soulmate I never wished for

tethered indefinitely, it seems

its impending grip upon me
I've battled heaven and earth to break
but while some days, I wish it all away
to take a diminutive breath, at least
other days, I pray it stays
as a reminder

a curse of imperfection.

oven psychic

there's a scar
on my forearm, closer to my wrist
arrogant among the freckle groves
where the top of the oven greets my flesh
every few months or so

a burn upon a burn upon a burn
bemusing to even the dwelling shadows
how an organ so tortured and battered
insists on reviving itself again

the wounds form instantaneously
seared and branded, enticing stares
a clotted crust that craves attention
from the past, flaking menacingly

taunting my patience for weeks on end
until the mark begins to cool
from crimson rage to plum to rose
a permanent blip on my ivory canvas

and yet, I never seem to learn
I forgo the risk of the same misjudgment
minimize the scorch despite its scar
a toxic relic of these shadowing times

upon my skin
upon my heart
upon my soul
neverending—

at least, it was.

through their eyes

you strive to stroke her skin
to rid a chill, to bring her back
beneath the glow of morning sun
to conjure blood across her cheeks

behind a jagged shadow wall
you pray she'll find a weakened spot
to strike a tear into your world
to nurse the breeze across her face

wake up (you cry) *please, wake up*
she tumbles further from your grasp
through clammy fingers, down a hole
the stranger slowly taking form

you try to salvage what you can
frantically tugging wiry roots
bits of hair and fingernails
matted to your shaking palms

you wait

to see if she saves herself
to see if the stranger sets her free
to watch the darkness clear away
its unpredictable nature reigns

you press your ear to sinking dirt
surrounding the space you saw her last
till scratches burst your eardrums
as she scales these crumbling walls

emerging bright as morning dew
a gasp of relief greets sweetened air
the stranger never takes her long
and life returns to blissful ballads

she's here now, life resumes
but deep inside, *it* lingers still
a dooming thought, a burrowing fear
of what could happen if one day

the stranger rises.

darkness warms

I have no energy left to be scared

the dark was terrifying to me as a child
I ran from it whenever I could
I screamed if light failed to illuminate
every corner of my ballerina walls
the crevices of a hobby stuffed closet
or the bubble floors along the hall
the living room with the pine green carpet
was always swallowed in the night
I could never make it to the stove light
shining refuge down below

but I'm too tired now
to fear the dark that closes in
I reach out with steady arms
to feel a prick
a mass
anything

I'm too tired to be scared of the dark
I'm too lonely to be scared of the dark.

hope breaks

a battle ensues to catch the light
before the sunset

I push the weakened shadows to the side
propelling towards the last rays
breaking through to gasp the air
pausing for me
still and silent

it's not a cure
the shadow curtains do fall again

but these raw wisps of hope
dance fairy air into my lungs
piercing slivers of golden light
through rings around my pupils
enough to wish for safety

for the first time
in a long time.

cellophane

in half a lunar cycle past
my shadows resemble cellophane
poorly packing my body behind cheap filters

now, a thin transparent sheet
untethered edges, crinkling away
despite the synthetic scars it seared into my skin

shaking fingers excoriate
the vestiges of life within
the film that has absorbed me through its pores

I gauge deep slits beneath my eyes
to catch a glimpse of what's beyond
gazing over tiny pools of tears filling the folds

a horizon unencumbered
by any shades or hints of gray
a breeze that bears no spikes in swaying trees

what cling remains behind, I tear
the shadow that stole my precious time
away from all of those I loved

with hope etched on my wrist, I dare to

breathe

I lay among the patchy grass
minding not its brittle touch
allowing ice-charged puffs of air
to surge and linger in my lungs
and little specks of cellophane
that stick still to my fingers
melt in the resurrection
of my resilience
and revenge.

Phase 3:
Light

disecting delusions

how could the whole world be against
one person, as the shadows whisper—

so intertwined in intimate affairs
crafting calculated cunning tricks
to annihilate every success a person achieves
dares to ponder
slinking around in the darkness
biding time to strike you down
at any moment
fibs sprouting on fabrications
to keep you
stuck

delusions—clearly
ridiculous to label truth in the light
but I believe it all in the shadows
as reality
as real as the hand that yields this pen
the whispers I placed upon my son's cheeks—

the world is out to get me
and I, not quick enough to escape
or stealthy enough to dodge
the wrath of lingering tricksters

feigning indifference to love

to evade loss

elusive stories to illuminate lies

shielding desires to deter jaded responses

ceasing to live

a life

so they'd have nothing to steal

even now, after decades of fighting
these delusions resurface
in hopes of grasping a gullible string
of a delayed following
silly thoughts for one in the light

but when the world is out to get you

for so long

reframing becomes a challenge

and I never leave a room

without looking over my shoulder

healing from delusions lasts

forever.

dreams are beautiful

from a distance
like a waterfall at its thunderous base
a labor of limitless force
dense compounding walls
trapping daring dreamers
in a tumultuous pool

a battle ensues
beating back frothy surges
seeking stray bubbles to siphon
the caving pressure of onlookers
plunging you deeper into the ravine
churning and tumbling bodies
among a relentless current
of doubt and insecurities

but take a second
to be still
beneath the weight
of never-ending falls
for there's such beauty
at the base of a dream

mossy stones, velvet to touch
shimmering fish that hold the sun
rainbow mists, glistening stones
a veiled world unlike any other
waiting among the shallows

drift a bit, past the fear
into careless tiered cascades
where worries cease to hold
permitting you to float
finally savoring the journey.

stop on red

the maple leaves draw me in
their bright red tips glowing among giants
dipped in the blood of a season
known to set my heart a flame

I've missed so many autumns
my soul, trapped in shadowy days

      yearning for the crispy gale
      to fluster illuminated landscapes
      swept away before I had a thought
      to relish in their glory
      leaves carving twisted paths, so swift
      they swirled into snowflakes before my eyes
      smothering my nose in icy bites
      shattering the curtain to reveal
      bare trees now left wanting
      crying out with gangling arms
      a reminder of what escaped me
      again

if only time would stop on red
as we do
at least to allow us a chance
to view the wonder it creates
savor the drips of transformation.

grating records

apologies so hollow and unkept
spit in fear
a phrase I've come to despise

like a broken record
flaking on the turntable
with a dragging needle
an ungodly screech
playing the same song
habitually, it's become
you still attempt to dance along
piercing my ears
with distractions and lies
swaying chaotically
a clown in a show
anything to change my mind
not the album
even though the vinyl's warped
you mimic steps before you invite
the composer
whose smile invariably fades
with the slightest critique
of the tune.

tear boobytraps

I'm tired of tears masking
as my resolution to conflict

a lack of predictability
preemptively activates my tear ducts
notoriously
salt streams choking words
transparent walls shielding thoughts
they drip along the wires in my brain
sparking those who reason with
my lungs

when tears subside and face puddles dry
in the wake of the fog clouding my mind
shame ensues from their compliance
for accepting unworthy blame
I kick myself for shutting down
and allowing others to see my tears
as I surrender to their every will
in spite of them

but the days of conceding are almost over
I whisper to myself
in silent corners
with hammers and nails.

I used to hate the Spring

the stench of melting snow
releasing spores of moldy mulch
sunken in fuzzy white patched beds
my grassy sopping pile of a yard
a muddy maze of earthy funk
stinging my nostrils
making deciphering feces from the earth
impossible

dirty snow mounds plague the curbs
the drive, the ditch, the deck
neverending
laden with brown salt, coarse gravel, gasoline
with worry
of what was buried beneath the snow
when darkness reigned here

mountains of leaves half decomposed
cracked toys mutilated by plows
carcasses left to putrefy
former animal neighbors
a pessimist's playground
little beauty on the horizon
to grasp, and yet—

something has happened
it seems my sense of smell has evolved

pushing aside the revolting tang
of winter's death
overcoming the rot of mother's gifts
plucking the sweetest smells
simmering the dawn
of warmth
only they are allowed
to waft upon my sun-starved skin
smelling nothing of my life
before

I never savored the candied scents of Spring
until this moment
now, everything around me
carries the redolent scent

of freedom.

I almost forgot

the late Spring air erased my memory, for just a second
the fullness of the hydrangeas
intoxicated my nose below our window

I awoke in shame of what I'd decided
the smell of your shirt, jumbled with berry bliss
swirling with the aroma of petals, bursting new life
turned swiftly to

      a disconcerting touch

      a mocking one-line compliment

      grilling questions digging shallow holes

      gracing the surface, never breaching

      throwing us back into the same cyclone

      of weighing worth by stealing time

      debating whose was gold vs dirt

I almost forgot

how much I've grown among the darkness
my promises to the child and hidden desires
I befriended there
of change, of merit, of truth
those pesky blooms distracted my heart
I wasn't at all defeated
to see them slashed upon the mulch
consequences of your revenge
against my soul.

banishing the script

I no longer wish to please you
to have you in my corner
it was a little crowded here
anyway
what with all the painted smiles
and singsong lies
perusing along the water
on the crystal lake filled
with sunken promises
avoiding discovery

I'd rather sink beneath the scum
of truth
than ever bathe among your praise
any longer.

I knew I had been in the shadows too long

when your luminescent face emerged
streaming with tears from icy eyes that melt instead of freeze
a warming greyish blue like the ice flows of Great Lakes
floating down the canal in the dead of winter
simply wanting my body to fall into for comfort, consoling

they wouldn't let go this time

I had engrossed myself in these latest shadows,
cloaking them to fit my ever-changing figure
they felt warm as wool harvested from the backs of black sheep
lulling me in familiar clover tongues
filling my head with poetry
despite feeding on all I was

I let them win

from under the hood I spotted you, pleading
signaling an instinct not even shadows can ignore
but my arms could not reach your hand through the cloak
the shadows and my soul had become one
and peeling the wool meant stripping us both away

I wasn't ready

a loose strand exposed that shadow's weakness at the base
your small hands pulled, ever so gently
unraveling this hooded trap till I was free to wrap you
finding solace in your glowing hair and the spot
on your neck the shadows could never mask

I began to wake in the cloak when light was supposed to reign
it fell suddenly, at random, but the wool was not so warm
the poetry far less profound
the hood obstructed your beauty
clouding the blue in your tear-struck eyes
pinching my nose to ignore the escape button

I took the welcome mat away from the shadows
the novelty of darkened times
the comfort in numbness
the conditional love I was spewing
stepping clear away from decades of traps
stomping tainted wool with complete awareness
for what it was

the shadows are no longer my home
I seek no comfort there
I'd rather sing sweet songs to you
to let the breeze play with my cheeks
to build kingdoms in the sky and animal parades on the earth
to cake dirt under my fingernails and paint in every grain
I desire nothing more than to enjoy these lives I've grown
assigning no more value to these shadow destroyers, now—

just an old forgotten cloak
hung in the back of a musty closet
only brought out to remember
why it was buried back there
to begin with.

digging for self

dirt lines my linen pockets
remnants of mineral surprises
discovered on timeless afternoons
amid the uprooted maples
upheaving hidden treasures
created in the warmth
of peaceful darkness

I thumb away the earth
caked in crevices
too cavernous to touch
revealing the certifiable beauty
of my personal plunder
the intimate powers
they proudly possess

it's taken me a moment
to accept the woman beneath
to polish the paralyzing faults
into weapons worth enough
to stand up to your critiques

for even the dullest, uneven shale
holds value.

green

if I failed to notice

       the stark glow of summer grass

       eager buds bursting into velvety leaves

       the mass return of fluttering wings

       slinking beetles beneath skeletons of fall

       flourishing vines mapping ancient trunks

       the aromas of wild and careless petals

the green

I would never leave

       the dull limbo of this silence

       a night terror, free to roam the day

       one lacking texture, undeserving

       like disobliging glass obscuring my sight

       smudged by those desperate to escape

       trapped between the parallel of life and

the dark.

dangerously dull

did you really think you could dull me?
slaughter my creative desires
simmer my ferociousness
calm my anxiety to the point of nothing
a lifeless body
a muted soul

I think it would be good for you
you coax another sedative
my friend takes it in pieces
to silence red flags in the mind
it could really help your every day
to help with what exactly?
to calm you down a bit
calm down?
from life
from life?
from life

I knew it was the end
when your bubble tried to seal me in
falsely shield me from these shadows
that swirl within my dreams
simply to trap me in your own

maybe you forgot
or chose never to accept
that my darkest shadows
the ones detested most
were the product of your own creation.

there's a girl I once knew

the angry one
who lives among the books
and scattered paper memories
ones she cannot fathom parting with
leaky ballpoint pens form wirey jungles
outdated and lost and lonely
spalted oak slabs caked in candle wax
dripped in fits of rage
coffee stains, remnant scribbles
scratches gone against the grain
light so bright they blind your mind
sear your nerves and dull your pain
her words are harsh and thoughtless
booming frequently without a care
echoing through the hallways
gracing only innocent ears
consequences of simple mistakes
scars that cannot be erased
her desperation clouded
in damning loathing statements
to ask for wishes that can't come true
her expectations unachievable

there's a girl I once knew
who visits me still
but at least I have become strong enough
to cast her away to dust.

mother moon

I've never felt so close to the moon
until I searched for hope

I too am a ghostly figure
lost among the clouds
hovering
purposefully over energy fields
gently pulling invisible forces

an orb guiding journeys
ebbing and flowing through lives
like the tides that burden the sea
unnoticed, unappreciated
except by those with lunar values

I come alive
when darkness falls
brightening in solidarity
unapologetically free
the pressure suppressed
the gazes put to rest

phasing through
these grueling days
I shine among these ancient stars
exposing the shadows
for every flaw they hide

when I'm new
        I yearn to grow
when I'm full
        my reign is everlasting.

owl soul

you're not supposed to be here
you waste your love on bystanders
who refuse to understand
who see your darkness as peculiar
a malfunction needing repair

and while, surely, it's uncomfortable
threatening at times
these shadows are ingrained in ways
you will never fully comprehend
a force that would cripple fragile pieces
if ever menacingly plucked away

I'm sad for you, sometimes
when misjudgment gives way to silence
censors the creativity seeping to the surface
only to be wiped away by damp rags
good intentions masked by closed minds

I never realized how powerful you were
until the night I heard the owls speak
their calls echoed through the valley
right when needed most
when the moon was black
and the clouds grew scarce
they sung with such conviction
confidence

an ode, if you will
an ode to your survival.

crow temptations

a crow sits above my head—again
looking down from the giant maple
watching or guarding, blessing or cursing
his purpose is never clear

he sits in silence—briefly—appearing from nothing
with muted flapping wings
till he calls to me, cackling, cawing
a clamor I cannot shake

through the veil more crows emerge
discussing worldly views, debating my fate
swirling manically in the vibrations of echoes
enticing one another with meddling tricks

the sun blinds my eyes as I watch
these resounding gods of the sky
relentless—every ounce of my attention
egging on their show

a crowd of one is enough
to boost and fill the cups of the cast
greedily spilling pride on branches
containing stubborn leaves

they lap up every drip
for waste doesn't exist in this murder
when my attention fades for a moment,
they disappear, disappointed.

my friend
you are not broken
you are not worthless
you are not a waste
you are not invisible

you're just in the shadows
temporarily
a dark blip in your reality
that will try to tear you apart

but you won't let it
you're an unyielding force
more real and ferocious than
any monster in the shadows

you can break through
you will—be patient
and always look for hints
of the light beyond the blackness.

About the Author

Shell Sherwood is a Midwestern-raised poet and writer now living on the East Coast, where she writes from her home in the Hudson Valley. Her poetry is shaped by her earlier work as a social worker, the transformative experience of motherhood, her passion for women's wellness and energy work, and a deep connection to nature and the Divine.

Shell is inspired by the darkness and resilience of humanity. This is her debut poetry collection, and she is currently working on future collections, children's books, and other projects. When not writing, Shell lives a creative and magical lifestyle with her children and partner.